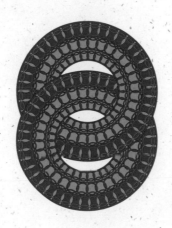

Life with Sam

Life with Sam

POEMS BY ELIZABETH HALL HUTNER

PHOTOGRAPHS BY SIMEON HUTNER

CavanKerry ❖ Press LTD.

Library of Congress Cataloging-in-Publication Data

Hutner, Elizabeth Hall, 1955–2002
Life with Sam : poems / by Elizabeth Hall Hutner ;
photographs by Simeon Hutner.
p. cm.
ISBN 0-9707186-5-9
1. Children—Death—Poetry. 2. Mothers and sons—Poetry.
3. Sick children—Poetry. 4. Grief—Poetry.
I. Hutner, Simeon, 1959–   II. Title.
PS3608.U86 L54 2002
811'.6—dc21   2002073729

Cover and book design by Sylvia Frezzolini Severance

FIRST EDITION

CavanKerry Press LTD
Fort Lee, New Jersey
www.cavankerrypress.org

For Bill

Contents

Foreword

by Rafael Campo

In one photograph, partly cut off at the left margin, a bouquet of wildflowers in a ceramic vase has begun to wilt—although it is not entirely visible, and it is dying, still the gathered blossoms remain beautiful. In the foreground, we see a little boy, adorable, half-smiling, his hand partly hidden in his bowl, as his mother the poet looks on forlornly. Stylized figures dance out-of-focus in the Oriental prints that hang on the room's wall behind the spare table; a mirror is hung between them, in which nothing is reflected. *Life goes on*, the contorted figures seem to say, despite the unfolding tragedy before us: we are not in for an easy ride. As we go on to read the mother's poems collected here, we learn that Sam, the boy in these accompanying photographs, is dying of leukemia. Like the cut flowers on their table, he is fading fast, a life foreshortened, barely glimpsed, and yet he is full of joy, colorful, vibrant, alive. Indeed, he lives on in his mother's words, and in the interspersed photographs taken by his uncle, in this incredible book *Life with Sam.*

I say "incredible" purposefully, because it is hard to believe that poetry today can still be so genuinely written in the spirit of healing, true to its origins as an indispensable mode for human connection. We live in a fragmented, anti-empathic moment: we have shock television to show us how hateful we have become, we have a war on terrorism that surely has killed more innocents than "evil-doers," we have a democracy that can be too easily hijacked and made to serve the interests of the wealthy and powerful while it fails to protect its marginalized minorities. And in our society's microcosm of the literary world, whose shrinking relevance itself would seem to be a victim of our increasing alienation from one another, we even encounter poets who write so obscurely, so preciously, that only super-specialized academics can understand their work. What to make, then, of Elizabeth Hall Hutner, who has the courage to reveal her very soul to us, who makes poems whose plaintive grief weighs on us like heavy stones on our hearts? Can one briefly shared life story, especially that of a small child, matter? Can such pain, raw and unimaginable and plainly told, be real? And can the gesture to articulate it be trusted?

As I read this book over and over again, the tears welling in my eyes answered for me: yes, here is a life and a poetry that does matter, that *must* matter, perhaps even more for its refusal of the banal, the sensational, the cynical and nihilistic. Hutner's large-hearted work joins her not only with the greatest parent-elegists of lost sons—Ben Jonson, Ralph Waldo Emerson—but also with a poetics older even than Horace, whose graceful and timeless lines she quotes in her own introduction to this book. Reading these poems, whose rhythms pound as hotly and audibly as the emaciated boy's heart against his mother's ear, whose memorable rhymes are like watermarks of tears on every page, we are returned to the purest, most elemental beginnings of poetry. Faced with the dread incurable disease, like the shamans in Native American cultures who had no chemotherapy or gamma radiation to offer the afflicted, the survivor turns to incantatory language for her healing balm; and though Sam has died, through his mother's poems he lives on, in a miraculous feat of immortality that all the powerful technologies of modern medicine failed to achieve. In a very tangible sense, this book cures cancer, even though in the end its hero succumbs; by speaking eloquently in the face of the awesome destructive power of this disease, by gazing fearlessly into its terrible beauty, by taming it imaginatively in celebrating the life of a boy who was never afraid to die in its grip, we can all find the kind of solace that we need to go on.

One such poem among the many here that risk so much and yield such great rewards is "Visitation":

He still comes to me at night as I sleep,
just as he did before we buried him—
not him, but the shell of his body, his sweet
presence gone before in the morning's dim
light. "You did such a good job," I whispered
then, as if he could hear me, and I think
he did because he comes back unheard
and unseen by anyone—at the brink
of dreams, we meet. "It's Sam!" he says in my ear
(as if I did not know). But I am slow
to understand everything that I hear,
see and feel, the hug he gives before he goes—
I feel it! I see him run toward me first
as he never could in life, a burst
of energy as he comes with such a smile,
he is here, my child, at night, for a little while.

What we notice first, perhaps, is that the poet has written a sonnet, our most traditional love poem, to describe what is both a harrowing and yet an oddly comforting encounter with her dead son; perhaps it is the choice of the familiar sonnet form that reassures us, invites us to experience this apparition not with horror but with tenderness and affection. Even the poet's choice of words connotes gentleness, the kind of unadorned language we might use in speaking to a child. Yet this poem is not so simple in what it performs: its heartbeat conjures Sam's physical presence, as do the playful, almost bounding rhymes. The ironic humor of Sam shouting out his presence—that proud proclamation of identity that we've all heard from kids— is only heightened by his ghostliness in the poem. Yet somehow, in that last binding couplet, the poet has resurrected her son, and is enjoying him again in an unspoken but deeply felt embrace.

If these finely wrought poems carry out the dual function of both containing emotion and by doing so paradoxically heightening it, then the photographs by Sam's uncle Simeon Hutner provide yet another dimension to this difficult, utterly absorbing narrative. Their own structure, as expressed in the fundamentals of their lighting and composition, also gives shape to what we come to understand as Sam's tenuous yet vital place in the world; as with the poems, what is left out is often as important as what is kept in. In one photograph, Sam looks mischievously over his shoulder, his mother but a blur amidst other objects in the background (hearth, books on shelves, rocking horse), as if to remind us who is the enduring central character in this story; we can almost hear him speak in this image, eager to have his voice heard, too, while all else is inconsequential. In another, toward the end of the book, Sam and his mother walk away from us down a long hospital corridor, hands clasped, his shiny bald head faintly lit by the brightness of a distant window, as if he has already begun departing this world, soul ready for its great leap out toward the absolute.

As I struggled with how I might find the words to introduce this unusual volume of extraordinary poems, amplified in its accomplishment and heartache by its internal dialogue with such unflinching photographs—like being asked to speak at a child's funeral, bemoaned one friend—I found myself seeking more poetry to make sense of my feelings, elegies in particular, which I have found so useful in my own work with patients who have had to confront the end of life. Few, I found, had the wherewithal to approach death with the up-close, honest immediacy of the Hutners; fewer still seemed capable of the brilliant clarity here, the ability to express such searing emotion without resorting to the release of sentiment or, on the other hand, the shield of overintellectualized distance. Yet I did return to Emerson, in whose long poem "Threnody" there are the following lines:

Was there no star that could be sent,
No watcher in the firmament,
Could stoop to heal that only child
And keep the blossom of the earth?
The eager fate which carried thee
Took the largest part of me.

Such is the kind of grief, total and unrelenting, that a parent who loses a child feels. There is no way around it. Perhaps no art, no mere act of creation can ever fill such a void. But it is to poetry, visual and linguistic, such as what constitutes this brave and humane *Life with Sam,* where we must turn to try.

Fall, 2002
Boston, Massachusetts

All mankinde is of one Author, and is one volume;
when one Man dies, one Chapter is not torne out of the booke,
but translated into a better language;
and every Chapter must be so translated.

—John Donne, *Devotions*

S omeone very dear to Sam and me once pointed out that being born and dying are the most intimate experiences two people can share—and that I had the privilege of being with my son through both. Sam was my first child and the child of my first marriage. This book grew out of our relationship, and it remains a document to that love.

One of the unexpected consequences of being a mother helping her son to meet the end of his life was a kind of closeness I had never before experienced. I found that I did not need pity. All mothers who suffer a child's death must, to survive, open their hearts in ways both profound and surprising. With the pain comes the deepest kind of learning.

A child who is dying does not need pity either, but instead merits the kind of honor we give to all great heroes. Having lived with Sam through almost four years of illness, I know he was heroic. He spent hours mastering his fate in his play with a Superman figure or in his watching on video, again and again, the story of Pinocchio, a puppet who undergoes a transformation from doll to real boy. Sam was very much a real boy. He knew the truth about his condition long before we accepted it, and one day he stopped what he was doing to say, "I feel dead, Mommy—" He fought hard to stay with us, but he knew he didn't have much time.

Sam is but one of many, many children who have lived out short lives with extraordinary grace and insight. I found comfort in knowing I was not alone— mothers of the 1800s were almost certain to lose a child, for the mortality rate then was fifty percent. No one could count on seeing all her offspring grow to adult-hood. Though the mortality rates have plummeted, children all around the world are still being lost. According to the Web site where I click to donate food each day, every 3.6 seconds someone dies of hunger and seventy-five percent of these people are children. In this country, cancer is one of the leading causes of death in child-hood, and many people I know have been touched by this reality. Not everyone loses a child to cancer, but a surprising number know someone who has, and many others know families with a child who has survived this illness. The death (or serious illness) of a child, though we so often turn away from its reality and so devoutly wish for it never to happen, is a part of life.

Though my son was so young, I often felt that he taught the adults around him about both suffering and grace. It was devastating to see him in pain, but it was equally uplifting to see him recover, again and again, from setbacks in treatment. I was often amazed as he simply picked up where he had left off weeks before when an infection put him in the hospital. He got on with living and learning as soon as he could, and he made up for lost time.

When Sam couldn't do something himself, he watched others do it. He loved cooking, woodworking, and painting shows on public TV. We used to watch them often together during long hospital stays. When he was well enough to visit a real woodshop, his delight in seeing the machines was deep and genuine. His response when we had to tell him the treatments no longer worked was entirely in character. "I'll just have to live with the leukemia," he decided. Sam met dying head-on, as he met all of life, and it became clear that for him, it was not some separate, secret thing; it was simply the next thing that he had to do.

He did not think only about himself, either. Once, he worried to his father's friend about how we, his parents, would manage if he didn't get better. Another time, hooked up to IVs, unable to speak because he was on a respirator, he looked over at my aunt who had come to visit him in the ICU and told her voicelessly, "I love you."

The standard wisdom on children and death is that children do not know much about it, but Sam taught me everything I now know about living and dying. And I think he taught his father too—because Sam's father was often with us even after we had separated, and Sam spent a lot of time at his father's apartment. Sam's dad, Alex, made many clinic visits, helped with home care, and stayed devotedly with his son through long nights at the hospital when I went home to rest. Sam and I also spent a great deal of time in the company of two wonderful women, one a college student who baby-sat and the other a terrific housekeeper. We all became family. My own family, too, came to our aid over and over again. My sister arranged birthday celebrations and visits and gave Sam her deep affection. Sam's grandparents provided the profound sympathy and love that could come from nowhere else. Simeon visited often and brought laughter with him. Sam was blessed in his other uncles as well, none more devoted than his Uncle Nico, who, with Alex, spent long, long hours at the hospital. All of us, so loved by Sam, were changed by him. One friend told me that when she thinks of Sam, she thinks of light.

Losing Sam is the saddest thing that has ever happened to me, but there were moments of joy right up to the end. In the stillness that surrounded Sam during his final days there was a peace and an acceptance unlike anything I could have imagined. We were closer in those last days than ever. As Sam grew sicker, he needed to know that his father and I would be all right no matter what and that we would stay by him forever. We told him these things, and we told the truth. Since then, I have found that the strength of my love for Sam has helped me navigate the almost unbelievable pain that followed his death. As years pass, that pain lessens and leaves the love intact.

Perhaps this is because Sam, in his short life, gave me the means to go on without him. As poets so often say, I found my voice. I began to write poems about our experience before he died, and I continued to write afterwards. I also took my experience playing guitar (which I learned when Sam was little in part to play for him), and I started to write songs. All during Sam's life I worked on a dissertation as well. I have spent years at it, given all the interruptions of illness, but I do not regret one second of that time. The poets I studied, John Donne and Horace, also brought great comfort. In Horace, I read one of the most extraordinarily compassionate poems on both the devastation of grief and the acceptance that comes after. He says to Virgil, who mourns the death of Quintilius,

> Suppose that you were able to play the lyre
> Even more skillfully than Orpheus played it,
> Causing the very trees to listen to him,
> What good would it do? Could the music restore
>
> Blood to the veins of the empty shade of one
> Who has died? How could the music persuade the god
> To open the door he has shut, and shut once and for all,
> The god whose horrid wand shepherds the dead
>
> To where they are going down there to be shut away?
> It is hard. But all of this must be endured,
> And by endurance what can never be changed
> Will be at last made easier in the heart.

> (Trans. David Ferry)

It is Horace's last lines that speak so eloquently to the sorrow. When he says, "It is hard," he uses one word, *durum*. The line stops completely here. There is nothing more to say. And it is only patience, *patientia*, the long suffering of grief, that finally leads to release. With Sam's life and death, I join the ancient poet in the expression of my grief. There is profound solace in his company.

Life with Sam

Spiritual Teacher

I thought you would be older than I am.
I thought I would recognize the classroom.
I was sure that every day you would say something I couldn't understand.
I expected that it would take years to figure out what you meant.
I thought I'd have to travel far away to find you.
I expected mountains and sky and only the devoted around you.

Instead you were little but strong.
I didn't go anywhere to meet you because you came to me.
At first, you took what you needed and didn't even say thank you.
I had to teach you.
You couldn't even speak in the beginning.
And once you learned, you had the questions.
In clinic one day, as I held you sleeping in my lap
After a procedure, one of the doctors stopped and said,
You look like the *Pietà 2*.

This wasn't what I expected at all.
I never knew I could love anyone so much.
I never believed my child could die before me.
I never thought we would spend most of our time together in the hospital.
I didn't expect you to look at me with eternity in your eyes.
I didn't expect the light around us when I looked at you.

Getting Ready to Go

During the last month of my pregnancy,
I sat outside in my parents' yard
in the green flowered dress I wore,
and felt the sheer size of my belly.
I had a bag packed for the hospital
with a nightgown, brush and comb, a book
to read. I was not sure what you would need,
so your grandmother bought you clothes
and brought them to the hospital
after you were born. When labor started,
we drove fast down the New Jersey turnpike
to the hospital in New York.

When you were three days old, we left
the hospital together. You were
collapsed in the car seat, your head drooping
like a heavy flower, too small
to sit alone, and I wanted to hold you.
I had packed your new baby clothes, my nursing dress,
diapers, the plastic pitcher and basin
the hospital gave me, and walked, unsteady,
back to the car to drive to New Jersey again.
I had bottles of water, a pacifier,
a bassinet for you to sleep in, but
I had no idea how to take care of you.

By the time you were six months, we could
travel anywhere. I packed up your clothes,
the little shirts and sweaters and pajamas,
and took you to see family in Vermont.
In the picture on my bureau, we are
lying in the hammock there as I smile
at you, you look toward the camera,
and Mooslamoo, the nearby mountain,
rises behind us in the blue sky.

When you could walk, you had a blanket you loved
and toys to bring with you wherever we went.
And then you were sick with leukemia.
I made a packing list so I would not forget
your medications, dressing kits, heparin flush.
I bought a plastic case with a compartment
for each day of the week, so I could
count out your pills, and a big, blue bag
to hold the blanket, the toys and the videos.
We went to the clinic or the hospital,
not to family, for most holidays.
Now, I have no pills or kits to count,
and everything else stays with me here.
So I choose your favorite sheet
to put under you, and a long-sleeved
shirt, striped, that I dressed you in many times.
I find the sweatpants to match and your shoes
black and shiny, leather, the only kind
you would let me buy. I pick out a toy train,
Thomas the Tank Engine, the old one
you loved best, and I include a book
and the rings I gave you to take
as something of mine to comfort you.
But how to part with the old blanket—
I bury my face in it for the smell
of you still alive, and put it with the rest.

When the bag is packed, I am ready to go.
We meet the undertaker at the funeral
home in New Jersey. "Here are Sam's things,"
I tell him. "Please be careful of the rings."
He sets the rings on his desk as we make
arrangements, and I hand him the bag of clothes
before I leave. Someone else will dress you,
put your toy, your book, and your blanket beside you
while I ride home to Brooklyn.

Diagnosis: Leukemia

You started preschool that fall.
I walked you to the old brick building,
and left you in the morning.
I noticed the bruises in October.
They covered your legs,
black, strange.
"He's two," I thought,
"and he falls all the time."
You had ear infections,
bronchitis, high fevers.
I gave you cool baths,
Tylenol, antibiotics.
In November, we had a conference
with your teachers. They said,
"He's behind the others. He doesn't
move enough. Can you put
play equipment in your house?"
Just before Christmas, I came home
from my shopping and you were gone.
Your father called and said,
"We're at the doctor's office.
Sam has a high fever, a cough.
We have to go to the hospital."
In the emergency room,
doctors hooked you up to an IV,
drew your blood, went over
every inch of your body.
"Have you noticed these petechiae before?"
they asked. Little, broken blood vessels.
At three a.m., the hematology-oncology fellow
came to our room to talk to us.
"The blood counts are abnormal. It could
be a virus, but it might be leukemia."
At noon the next day,
they did a bone marrow.

When the surgeon came in the afternoon
to find the little boy who needed
a catheter for chemotherapy,
we knew.

Grieving

"Now that I have a child of my own,
  a friend writes, "I understand your loss."
"No," I think, "now you understand
  what I had."

                              Do you
remember how we used to lie together
on this couch or on the hospital bed
and watch TV? Why am I talking to you?
You seem so close though you are gone.
Yan Can Cook, *The Yankee New Workshop*
(you always reversed the words),
Mathnet, you liked Channel Thirteen.
Each day on the painting show, the artist
painted a new landscape right before
our eyes. I ordered the books
from the cooking shows, but you died
before we could cook anything.

At the clinic, the TV was on all day.
The nurses watched soap operas
even though all the patients were children.
"There's Carlo!" you told me. "I'm scared of him."
He was a villain plotting a murder.
We asked for the VCR and watched
Thomas the Tank Engine or *The Wind
in the Willows* instead. Other children
wanted to see them too. We moved the machine,
and they adjusted the poles and hooks
that held their IV medications
so everyone could see. Sometimes,
at the end of the day, we saw *Sesame Street*
or *Carmen Sandiego* on the big TV,
and you cried if anyone changed the channel.
No one else seemed to like public television

except for one doctor who thought it was
educational. She was the one
who said, "Spit, spot!" just like Mary Poppins
when you needed to take a shot,
be examined, or have a bone marrow.
After she had been in the clinic awhile,
she smiled or asked how we were instead.

You saw *Star Wars* so often you could
talk just like the alien creatures.
Your stepfather made you every weapon
and spaceship in the movie. He drew each one first,
asked, "Is this what you want?" and if you nodded
"Yes," he fashioned it out of toilet paper rolls,
cardboard boxes, packing tape, corks and chopsticks.
We bought or rented all the fairy tales.
I loved *Cinderella* and *Sleeping Beauty*,
but your last days in the hospital, you watched
Pinocchio, all about the doll
who came to life as a little boy
after he learned to tell the truth.

You always told the truth, but sometimes,
in the last days, you did not want to talk at all.
You were past playing with your models,
so we turned on *Pinocchio* again.
I could no longer lie next to you
and hold you in my arms. You hurt too much.
I sat beside the bed and watched and prayed.
I too would have gone into the belly
of a whale, just like Pinocchio's father,
if I thought that I could save you.

My friend does not know what happened
after we took you home. That night,
as you felt your strength leaving you,
you said, "Maybe we should watch a video."
"No," I told you, "it's time for sleep."

We carried you upstairs. In the morning,
after you died, the doorbell rang.
UPS had brought us a package,
Disney movies from my aunt out West.
Now we had every one available,
a complete set.

I Grow My Hair

When I washed my hair this morning, I
remembered I had decided to grow it
when you were in the hospital the first time.
I comb it out carefully and check
its length in the mirror. Heavy, brown,
it covers me like a blanket.
When I see friends after a long time,
"Your hair has grown so long," they say.
"I know," I tell them, "I always wanted
hair so long I could sit on it."
You were born with hair, and people used to say,
"Oh, your baby has so much hair!"
I was so proud of you I kept
a baby curl in my jewelry box.
As you grew, your hair turned blond, the curls
covering your neck and ears, adorable.
After you were diagnosed, we asked,
"Will his hair fall out?"
"Yes," the doctor told us, "in about three weeks."
We took you home from the hospital,
and your hair came out in handfuls. I found it
on your pillow every morning.
A few stray wisps were all that you had left.
Later, when the chemo lightened, it came back,
so we went to the children's barber
on Madison Avenue. I kept a lock
of that hair too. You relapsed
and were bald again.
My bangs had grown out by then;
the rest fell down my back. You played with it,
and smiled when I wore it loose.
"You look beautiful, Mommy," you would tell me.
When you relapsed, the doctors put a bulb-like
syringe into your scalp to deliver

the medicine to the fluid around
your brain and spine, the site of your relapse.
Your head, shaped, I always thought, like the head
of a Roman in one of those ancient sculptures,
now had a permanent bump and scar,
but a fine, dark down grew to soften it.
The second time you relapsed, you kept
your hair despite the high dose chemo.
When you did not go into remission,
I was not surprised.
At the end, with experimental chemo,
your hair fell out again.
"Good!" my father said when I called him.
"Maybe the chemo will work this time."
We had hope as I brushed your hair off
my clothes, my hands.
I could not brush it off your head as
your father did. He brushed and washed until
you were bald again. I cried, but we
scheduled you for a bone marrow transplant.
Our social worker said, "Now you have your chance."
The cancer came back after the final treatment,
so we took you home to die in your own bed.
The nurse said, "This room is dark. We should
move him back downstairs in the morning."
The windowpane above the air conditioner
was defective, fogged over. I never
could fix it. Morning came, but you had died,
your head, beautiful and bare, turned
toward the window and the world you could not see.

A Reason to Write

You would have been nine years old on Monday
when we went to your grave to plant flowers,
the only present I could give to you.
But here, I can return to you, age six.
I have been out in Manhattan all day,
a guitar lesson in the Village, a stop
for lunch, and before the subway home,
I buy the Brio train you want for your set.
I like being out, shopping, away,
but you are sitting on the stoop with Debbie.
She says, "Sam missed you, so we came outside to wait.
There is curry on the stove for your dinner,
and Sam already ate his noodles and cheese."
Back upstairs, she puts on lipstick,
picks up her purse, checks for subway tokens
as I step over the train tracks you and she
have set in an elaborate arrangement
across the living room floor. "I found it!"
I tell you and give you the bag to open.
"Debbie, look—my new engine!" and you
add it to the train cars already on the tracks
as she smiles then says good-bye, "See you
tomorrow, my friend," and goes out the door
for the long subway ride home. You and I
lie on the couch together as she rides.
We watch your shows on Channel Thirteen
until you get up to play with Ninja turtles.
"Mom," you ask, "where is my turtle's sword?"
We find it, you play, we put away
the turtles and the trains for the night.
Upstairs, after we put on your pajamas
and flush your broviac—the chest tube
you've had since diagnosis—after I
carefully place the needles and tubes
in the discard container on the shelf of my closet,

I read you the stories of Mr. Muddle
and Mr. Bump. "Bump!" you say when I pause
for the word in Mr. Bump's story.
You fall asleep in my arms, and I
go over the day in my mind. The dressing
at the catheter site has been changed,
you've had all your pills, I carefully cleaned
the broviac before putting in the needle
to flush. Your blood counts are good, no fevers.
So I gently slide my arm out
from under your head, kiss you, and go
downstairs to have my dinner.

Waiting to Speak

You never spoke the way a toddler does—
Made up words and mispronunciations.
You waited, and I think it was because
You needed everything in right relation.
When you spoke, long after others started,
Your words were perfect, sentences complete.
You took a thought, went right to where the heart is
Deep in feeling, simple and discreet.
And I began to write about this time
to fight against a silence so profound
I heard ringing in my ears, the grinding
of my teeth, minutiae of sound.
We grew together learning this new world,
Words tumbled, rose above our heads and swirled.

Words tumbled, rose above our heads and swirled.
We watched them shiver in the summer air.
They shimmered like the bubbles our breath whirled
Away from where we sat out on the stairs.
The bubbles, evanescent, that we blew,
Floated up, soap rainbows in their sides.
They formed on plastic wands and slowly grew
Until, caught in the light, they came alive.
You sat so often on that stoop with me,
Or with the sitter until I returned.
And from those stairs with such economy
Of will you searched the street until you learned
Just where and when I might appear at dusk.
You leaned into the night, eyes filled with trust.

You leaned into the night, eyes full of trust,
Expecting me, your mother, to come home.
Repeated to yourself, she must, she must—
You knew me. I could not leave you alone.
I, on the other hand, felt less secure.
I rarely let you wander out of sight.
I needed you beside me to be sure
That you were safe, were real, would not take flight.
You seemed to be conversant with the air,
To hear its voices, sibilant but hollow.
They called to you—you turned but did not dare
to go with them because I could not follow.
I kept you here by simple force of will.
Imprisoned in my heartbeat, you stood still.

Imprisoned in my heartbeat, you stood still,
Stopped by the fright that lay inside my voice.
You held my hand in pity, waited till
Your illness deepened leaving you no choice.
But long before leukemia ran wild
Inside your veins, we walked the Brooklyn Bridge.
You pushed your stroller by yourself and smiled,
Winning your way, though hard, in what you did.
You won. I watched you in admiration
As triumph radiated from your face.
This was no game but was a re-creation
Of other battles fought for time, for grace.
A war is won through forthright concentration.
The soldier stays. Love never leaves its station.

Do soldiers stay or can love leave its station?
I had no choice. I had to stay by you.
I was not fit—I had so little patience—
And yet, I learned by instinct what to do.
I walked the hospital halls late at night
to let you sleep until the nurse came in.
She took your temperature, turned on a light
that woke you, fixed monitors on your skin
So delicate—so soon past babyhood.
I wanted to leave. I longed to take you home
But I followed protocols, hoped they could
Bring you through leukemia on their own.
They could not do it. We lost what life we had—
Irreplaceable and profoundly sad.

Irreplaceable. I, profoundly sad,
Although life blooms around me in a riot,
Watch while your brother plays—all that I have—
No matter how my restless need for quiet.
I've lost the central stillness of your life
In your last days, when vision lit your eyes
To radiance, to reckonings, what might
Have happened with such power to revise
What we were powerless to change. I yield
To the inevitable. When I do,
I'm caught in light that comes across the field
Outside our window. Rain ends. Something new
Will turn your brother's gaze, will make us one.
Today I see us, mother and her sons.

Today I saw a mother and her son,
A snapshot taken from a magazine.
I cried to think of what we had become.
My waiting hip won't carry you again.
But you still speak to me through little signs,
The kind of things that no one else would notice.
Today a train a small child leaves behind
Sits on the counter where I set my groceries.
Thomas the Tank Engine—I see your trains—
Your play serious, silence so intense—
You pushed them round the tracks—all that remains
Of you, a form of recompense
For loneliness, the tears before the pause—
You never spoke the way a toddler does.

Entering the Light

Nobody in New York ever has light.
In every apartment I looked at,
I always asked, "Is there enough sun
to grow anything?" I chose our last place
in Brooklyn because of all the windows,
three in the living room alone,
but we were surrounded by buildings.
The plants I bought at the hardware store
did not all survive.

The first time we went to the hospital,
I bought a basket of African violets.
My mother had had one when I was born.
The last, I found a Swedish ivy plant.
We started your last three months in a room
full of light. As the doctors tried the final
experimental treatments, I put toys
away at night, tucking them on the shelf
in front of the windows just as, at home,
I picked up toys after you went to bed.
I watered the ivy from a paper cup
I brought with your dinner from the Chinese
restaurant down the street.

Our old doctor went to Boston
and the new doctor sent us home
too soon. When we came back the next day,
we had to take a different room
with fewer windows, and they were blocked
by buildings, so the room was dark.
I had left the plant at home, of course.
The doctors tried more treatments while I looked
for a brighter room, and your stepfather
put together a small wooden helicopter
with a solar panel.

By the time I found a sunnier room,
you no longer ate the meals I brought you.
We moved across the hall anyway,
and the blades on the helicopter
spun all day long as you sat in the big, blue chair
or lay in your bed, eyes closed, resting.
While you slept, I read a book about children
who have almost died and have seen the light.
They said it was beautiful, and they said
they did not want to come back.

After you died, I moved to New Jersey
to the house we had planned to live in together.
It had eight windows in the living room
and was so full of the November light!
I hung our plants or set them on the bookshelf.
I put our couch by the windows too,
so I could lie there under your comforter
with its soft cover of clouds and stars,
and watch the blades of the helicopter
spin day after day in the sun.

The Children's Year

Parenting books take me through a yearly
schedule of holidays with suggestions
of what to do or to prepare. Clearly
they give their instructions. "Any questions?"
they ask, and "Yes," I answer, "I have one."
What do you do with a leukemic child?
I go through the year with this child, my son,
in memory. Christmas presents wait while
we hear the diagnosis, bring the tree,
artificial, small, to the hospital room.
Easter is heavy chemotherapy.
His birthday is relapse, clinic is school.
A Halloween costume is put away,
Though my sister asked for it one day
for her son. Thanksgiving comes a month after
the day he died. That is all I remember.

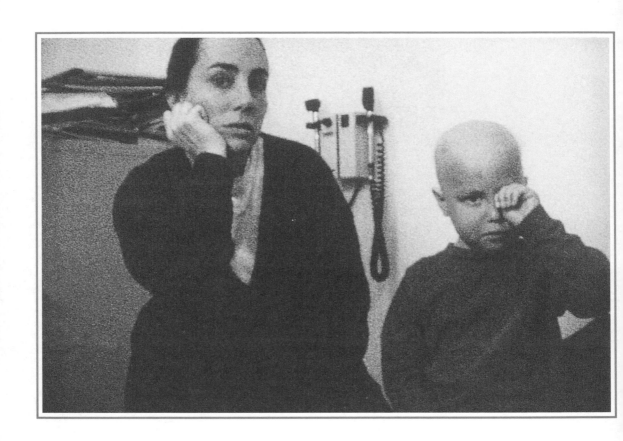

Waiting for Easter

Monday, Tuesday, Wednesday, I took Sam
to clinic. The doctor put the needle
into his scalp where the ommaya is placed
under the skin, a rubber bulb and tube
extending down to the fluid around the brain.
One, two, three, we counted together
before the procedure.
Then, spinal fluid came out into
the syringe, and Ara-C went in.

Thursday, I prepared for Easter.
I went to three different florists to find
the forsythia branches not yet in bloom.
Sam and I were too tired to blow the eggs,
so I hung the eggs we colored two years ago
when he was on maintenance chemotherapy,
able to go to preschool, able to play.

When my boyfriend came home, I said,
"Look, isn't it pretty?" He said, "Yes,
but when I was married, we had branches
in flower, and I made complicated
egg ornaments, models of planes and once,
the water tower from the old farm."
"I haven't time for all that!" I cried. "And
maybe you should go back to your wife
and your two girls who aren't sick like Sam."

Today, we go to clinic again.
It is Good Friday. The doctor says
Sam's chances for survival are fifty
to sixty percent. Sam needs a month
of radiation to the head and spine.
He will lose IQ and height. "It could be
worse," I think. I put away the image

of a son tall like his father and
intellectual like his father, like me.
The doctor says, "Think of the glass as half
full, not half empty," but I cannot.

I sit with Sam in the clinic afterward
as he gets the Cytoxan, an IV
that takes the rest of the day. We sit
with another boy who has a different
blood disease that is wasting his body away.
He has no hands anymore, and his skin
is full of sores. When he talks,
I have to force myself to look at him,
but Sam talks to him easily,
and says to me later with sadness,
"He's been that way since he was born, Mommy."
"Yes," I say, "I know." At the end of the day,
we say good-bye to the boy, the nurses,
the doctors, to go home for Easter.

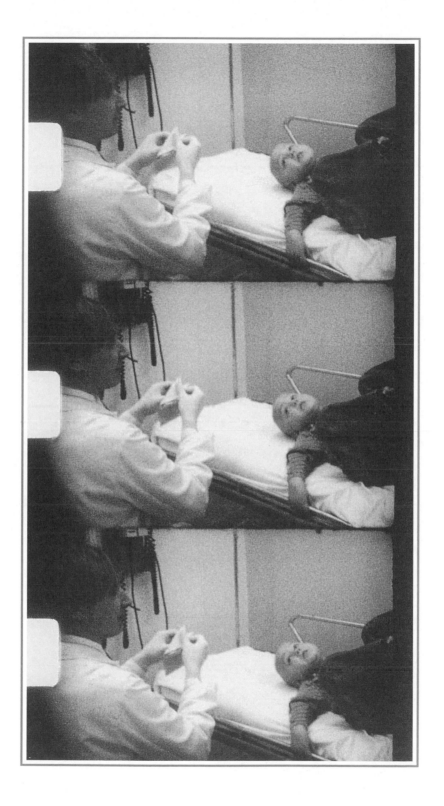

Stepfather

He sits beside you, cardboard in his hands—
"Which one?" he asks. You scrutinize the screen.
"That one!" He stops the tape to understand
How to build the spaceship you have seen.
He cuts the cardboard on the lines he's drawn
To make the wings, the body, guns and tail.
His strokes are sure. His hands move swiftly on
The task you've set him, sure he cannot fail.
He works beside your bed and lets you watch
All day while you are quiet but awake—
Then while you sleep he cuts a final notch
And tapes all tight, so strong it cannot break.
Next morning, as you hold it with a grin,
You ask him "Could you?" He begins again.

Relapse

Lately, at dark I wonder which is worse,
To go by dying and deserting you
Or watch you go without me, slowly, first.
Somehow, somehow, we try to make it through
tonight. Your bones are aching, and I know
Vincristine makes them hurt. "Oh Mom, my legs
Are breaking off!" you cry. I nod as though
Your bones can shatter like the shells of eggs.
You cough despite Intal and Proventil,
Then take the Prednisone prescribed this week.
Nothing I can do will help you heal.
You talk until you cry—now barely speak—
"Throw me in the garbage—let me be dead!"
Then—"It's just the pills that make me think that way."
I nod and when you look at me and say,
"I walk alone," I tuck you into bed.

The Cross

Today I nail my heart upon this cross
Since nothing hurts like hurt of losing him.
I offer up my hands and feet because
I am alive and must begin again.
You would not think that after years alone
The pain could haunt or tear me to the quick,
But it does. And with each nail I groan
As I am hoisted up, heart sore, soul sick.
As mother, I have given up my son,
Wrapped in my arms, to sickness and to death.
We breathed together, rose and fell as one,
Until he could no longer take a breath.
You who have not lost do not yet know
How infinite pain is, how sharp but slow.

Homemaking

Today, after I fold the clean clothes
and put away the napkins and towels,
I pick up *The Candlelighters' Newsletter*
for parents of children with cancer:
Light a candle, for a child, for hope.
I read the lead article, home care
for the pediatric cancer patient.
A nurse, a doctor, a social worker,
and a mother all give advice
on how to pick a home care agency.
Halfway through, I realize the nurse
is describing hospice care for the dying
child. I see you, surrounded by machines,
as you sat on the couch in our living room.
So many supplies! The oxygen tank
stood by the kitchen counter, alien.
We brought you home with a mask on your face,
portable oxygen at your feet in the car.
Our home nurse gave us papers to sign
while the technician showed us how to use
the bigger tank. "If he needs more oxygen,
change to this tank, go up on the dial."
The tank was so big, I thought, "We'll be here
for days." I wanted you to myself, but
instead, the house was full of people.
"I love you," you told your aunt as she left.
When everyone else had gone, the night nurse
came. She sat with you and your daddy
on the sofa. "I want to lie down with Mommy
in my own bed," you said and smiled.
"After supper," we told you, and your daddy
said, "Go eat. We'll be fine." Now I would tell
him, "No. I want my son. You go eat."
But then, because I thought you would live
at least another day, maybe another week,

I went to supper. When I came back,
you were breathing hard. We took you upstairs
for the night. I wanted to lie down with you
as we had promised, but tubes ran everywhere.
You couldn't breathe, even so, and when we
switched the tubes to the big tank, you closed
your eyes and fainted. "No!" "Sam!" "No!"
Your father, the nurse, and I called you back.
You came to us with an effort of will, of love.
You stayed for one last night.

I turn from the description of home care
to an article on rehabilitation
of cancer survivors who often have
learning disabilities from chemo
and radiation. The program sounds good,
and I think, "I should copy this
for Judy's son. He could use it."
I look at the correspondence section
where parents write, "We are thankful
for every day with our child. Every day,
every child is precious to us now."
Just before I put the paper down,
I come across the helpful hints.
"If you are having difficulty
cutting a pill in half," one mother writes,
"try cutting on a folded towel."

Change

How could I tell anyone what Sam saw?
"No one will believe me," I thought.
So until now, I have not said a word,
but as Sam lay in the hospital,
hardly in his body anymore,
he saw spirits. I had read about
how we should let the dying speak,
let the visions come unclouded by drugs,
but Sam shouted "No!" when they came,
so we told him, "They want to help you.
Let them come. Let them visit." He still refused,
and I got angry. "Let them come!"

Sam never liked changes. I had to tell him
about a trip to the clinic a day ahead.
"No shots, just a visit to the doctor,"
or, "You need a bone marrow test Monday."
Now, "That's my grandfather!" he said,
pointing from his bed to the hospital wall,
and I remembered a book that showed us
how to use our hands to make shadow pictures
on the wall, rabbits, dogs, whatever
you could imagine. Sam and I had tried it,
at home, with the glow of his nightlight.
But this wall was empty to me though
I knew his father's father who had died
years ago must be in the room with us.
"Of course," I thought, "he had to come!"

I still can see Sam though he has died.
He holds his grandfather's hand while he waits.
"If I go first," I told him in the hospital,
"you will come after. But if you go first,
I will follow." Then I read him once more
from *The Runaway Bunny* where the rabbit

mother becomes a tree or a fisherwoman
or even a human mother to follow
her child no matter what shape he takes
in his imagination.

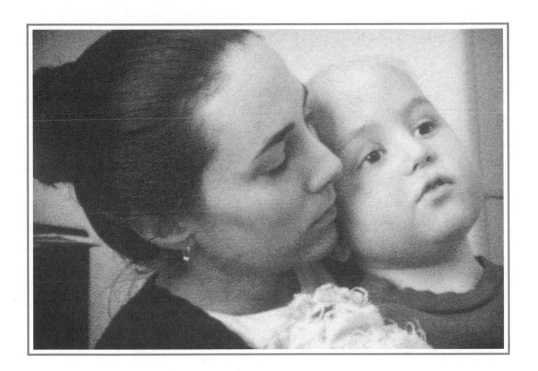

Your Name

Someone, inadvertent, speaks your name.
I startle like a deer caught in the light.
The world resolves to you, to Sam, the same
Miserable joy and I defy it
By conjuring your soul in bits and pieces:
Clothes or toys, old cards that friends once sent.
And when I see your name, something releases
Deep inside, a longing so intense
I cannot cry. My life cannot resume
Its ordinary tasks or daily rounds.
I stop to feel and tend this deepest wound
Of nothing left, no room that holds your sound.
So finally, have I become a mother?
First child gone. And will I have another?

Night

Turn out the light to let the nighttime in.
You, who were alone, find comfort now.
Embrace the air, whole heart, as if a friend
To trees whose shadows beckon without sound.
Some love the sun and breathe their best by day,
But I wait for a darker kind of light,
The night that holds me in its arms and plays
Until my soul uncurls in its delight.
I watch the car lights flicker on a wall—
I hear nocturnal sounds—an owl hoots—
Echoes of my sorrow in it all
As sadness settles down into its roots.
But cradled now, I don't care if I cry.
Night bows her head and does not ask me why.

Looking for His Grave

For the first two years, when I went
to the cemetery on Sam's birthday
or All Soul's, I walked past the grave.
I was looking for Sam.
I could not believe his body, grown
in mine, and held, bathed, clothed by me
was under the ground.
When I stood by the grave, I was overcome
with the desire to dig.
He did not need to be saved,
but I wanted to rescue him.

I looked for a small stone
because Sam was young and small
when he died. In my mind, I saw
a short, rounded stone like the older
gravestones in the cemetery,
the stones for children from the last
century, stones tucked next to parents
as a newborn is tucked in next
to his mother. The suffering!
Two or three infants and children
died in the families I wandered
among. I felt at home there.

But Sam was not buried with them.
His grave is in the new section
where the stones are bigger and fancier.
I see few children, few young women
who must have died in childbirth.
I recognize the grave of a man
who used to sell candy to us
from his wheelchair when we were
children. Sam is buried just
beyond him, under a stone polished

to a hard shine. It is basically
square, with what the cemetery
keeper calls "shoulders."

                Its shine
reminds me of Sam's father's shoes,
and the shoulders are his father's
in his grey lawyer's suit. The stone is tall,
taller than Sam, tall like Sam's father.
Sam loved to wear a tie like his father
and black shoes like his father,
but he wore the tie over his long-sleeved
t-shirt and the shoes with his sweatpants.
He liked to have a large square of bright
yellow cotton as a cape, knotted
around his neck, and when he went out,
he liked to keep his red wool coat
open, so he could pick up
the corners and fly with it.

Today, I went right to his grave.
I put down the flowers, and looked
at the boxwoods Sam's stepfather
has planted on each side of the stone.
I held the new baby in my arms,
and I cried as I read Sam's name.

Sam I Am

Yesterday,
As if just outside the room,
I felt you near.
I dropped into the trance
In which you used to play
With the toys that I have long since
Put away.

Later, the nurse came into my room
Carrying a basket of flowers.
After your stepfather read the card to me,
He turned it over,
And on the back was scribbled
In an anonymous hand,
Congratulations!!!!!

I looked out the hospital window then,
And everything became part of your toy world.
There was the bridge over the big river,
A roadway beside the water,
And travelling over all were boats,
Cars and trucks,
Here and yet remote.

Prayer

When I close my eyes, let me always
feel the ache under my breastbone
as it spreads down my belly to my legs,
out to my arms, to my fingers, my toes.
Let me remember my son just turned two,
hooked to a heart monitor, an IV
pumping medicine into his veins.
Let me let him go to surgery,
and let me let the machines take the place
of my arms. Let me watch the screens
instead of the rise and fall of his chest.
Let me be weak with sadness, let me cry
as I endure the separation.
I let him go, step by step, until he died.
I gave him the pills, I checked the blood counts,
I held his hand for the bone marrow tests.
I saw the little girl, healthy, who looked
away when she saw him, bald and dying,
in the X-ray room, but I have looked away
when the dying one was not my son.
Please let me also remember his voice
calling "Mom!" and his laugh as he ran to me
when I picked him up from preschool.
Let me feel the heaviness of his head
on my shoulder as he slept.
Even if it is only in memory,
let me hold his peaceful breathing
in my breath as the new baby grows
within me.

Other World

Maybe I have waited for disease
Carried by my blood into the bone
To offer me the chance I think I need
When life without you leaves me too alone.
Now I will suffer all that you endured
When doctors gave you needles, pills and fear.
And since for you, we never found a cure,
My illness is the thing that we can share.
If I catch a glimpse of where you are—
It tantalizes. What have I to lose?
No, I could go—it really isn't far.
Everything depends on what I choose.
But I have other loves for whom I stay.
I must turn back and let you slip away.

Visitation

He still comes to me at night as I sleep,
just as he did before we buried him—
not him, but the shell of his body, his sweet
presence gone before in the morning's dim
light. "You did such a good job," I whispered
then, as if he could hear me, and I think
he did because he comes back unheard
and unseen by anyone—at the brink
of dreams, we meet. "It's Sam!" he says in my ear
(as if I did not know). But I am slow
to understand everything that I hear,
see and feel, the hug he gives before he goes—
I feel it! I see him run toward me first
as he never could in life, a burst
of energy as he comes with such a smile,
he is here, my child, at night, for a little while.

Life keeps moving in spite of loss, though for a long time I felt I could not move at all. This was a strange and startling sensation. I who had studied modern dance seriously, walked all over Manhattan with books in a knapsack on my back, sprinted up subway steps, and staggered home under loads of groceries, became very, very still. I moved out of the city (something I had longed to do with Sam), but others packed my boxes. When I arrived in New Jersey and settled in a new little house, I spent hours on the couch where Sam and I once had snuggled together, and I looked out at the fields from under Sam's quilt with its soft flannel cover. I couldn't always answer the phone. I couldn't write. I cried when I saw a boy who reminded me of my son, and ambulances passing brought back the old agony.

Still, I had a beautiful puppy to train, a puppy who was meant to be Sam's friend but became my constant companion instead. We did get outside to walk the fields around the new house together. And I married Bill, the man whom I call Sam's stepfather in these poems. We had fallen in love years ago, parted through misunderstanding, and reunited during Sam's illness. He moved up from North Carolina to be with me and my son. At the end, there were three of us, me and both Alex and Bill, parenting in the hospital—and at home we worked together too. This unexpected partnership was a gift that Sam gave to us, an ability to transcend our own concerns in order to care for him.

A year after remarrying, my new husband and I had our own baby boy. My husband had said to me long before the pregnancy that he felt there was a child waiting for us, and when Will arrived, he looked at us so directly and was so completely here, so aware, that he did not seem a newborn at all. He had come to help us, I sometimes think, and so he has. These days, he plays with Sam's trains and the models that his father made for Sam in the hospital. There is a poignant comfort and continuity to this—and when Will asks if the toys are now his, I say yes without hesitation. Sam would want him to have them, I know.

Still the devastation has taken a long time to heal, and a year after Will's birth, I was diagnosed with breast cancer. The tumor was directly over my heart. I had to choose then whether I really wanted to live. I had the option of giving up this life and following Sam. I knew, though, that he would want me to stay, and I also felt

that I could not choose to inflict the kind of suffering I was passing through onto my husband and son. Finally, I realized that not just for anyone else, but for myself, I wanted to live. Sam's love gave me a sense of purpose, of worth, because for him I had done something I had never thought I had the strength to do. It was time to continue on without him in order to fulfill my own life's work.

So I went through the cancer experience a second time and found new ways to cope with it, including profound changes in my diet and the way I live my life. The most fundamental change was perhaps the hardest; I took responsibility for myself. I listened to everyone's advice, but I made my own decisions. I talked to more than one doctor. Eventually, I found alternatives to medicine to help me as well. This has been the key to my survival, this listening to the small, inner voice that serves as guide. As I regain my health, I am stronger than I was before becoming so ill.

My love of Sam has given me so many gifts that I cannot name them all. If asked to choose the most important, though, I would say it might be the strength which comes from connection. In Donne, I found the understanding of humanity that serious illness brings. In a passage from the *Devotions*, written about and during the poet's own sickness, he says,

> No man is an Iland, intire of it selfe; every man is a peece of the
> Continent, a part of the maine; if a Clod bee washed away by the Sea,
> Europe is the lesse, as well as if a Promontorie were. . . .

I was a loner before having a child and even during much of Sam's lifetime, but I am alone no longer. I believe in Sam's continued presence as spirit, for one thing. For another, I rely on an ever wider circle of friends who have over and over again come to my aid. And there is this book itself, a joint project with my brother, to prove how blest both Sam and I were (and I remain) in Simeon's steady and loyal affection. My father and mother, too, with their own courageous lives, have given me the examples of energy and determination I needed. Finally, my life depends on the love of my husband (who saved me by finding the tumor in the first place) and of my children, my son and stepdaughters. In their eyes, I am whole and I am beloved. There is no happiness greater than this.

ELIZABETH HALL HUTNER

Elizabeth Hall Hutner
died on November 30, 2002.

April 12, 2001, San Francisco

My sister Liz and I are the youngest of five children, and we have always had a close relationship. She is there in one of my earliest memories, sitting me down on the picnic table in the backyard and teaching me patiently how to tie my shoe. (The snapshot of us, above, with our housekeeper, Mrs. Cray, was taken around this time.) Later on, she was the first person to show me what a poem was; even in college, I remember calling her for advice on everything from girlfriends to a paper I was writing on Chaucer. As we got older, the difference in our ages seemed to diminish and we grew closer still, speaking often on the telephone and visiting frequently when we lived close enough to do so.

After I began taking photographs at the age of fourteen, Liz was an early, and frequent, subject. Years later, when she gave birth to Sam, it was only natural that I would document his life as well. I began making the photographs in this book with no other purpose, and when Sam became ill, I continued photographing the same way. It was only when the aggressiveness of Sam's cancer became apparent that I began approaching the photographs with a sense that they might be representations not simply of a childhood, but of an entire life.

Sam enjoyed being photographed and was so accustomed to it that it was almost second nature to him. Yet he also appreciated the significance of having his image recorded: if he was ever uncomfortable with the camera, or he didn't want to be photographed in a specific situation, he would motion for me to stop shooting and then let me know when it was okay to continue. I stopped taking photographs of Sam when his condition worsened and he was spending much of his time in the hospital.

After Sam's death, all the material that I shot went into storage. Every once in a while, Liz and I would discuss the idea of combining her writing with my photographs, but the subject was so painful that we hesitated to go ahead with the project. It was not until eight years after Sam's death that Liz sent me her poems. I found them beautiful and overwhelming at the same time, and they led me to see the photographs I had taken in a new light. Some of the photos that I was particularly fond of seemed less significant now, while others that I had overlooked took on new meaning. Soon I was scanning negatives, making new prints, and beginning to lay out this book.

It has been rewarding work. I have treasured the opportunity to collaborate with my sister on a project that could not be any closer to her heart. In reading the poems and working with the photographs, I also felt as if I was once again spending time with Sam, reliving the pain of his illness, but also his incredible strength and joy in life. It was a privilege to know him.

SIMEON HUTNER

Author's Acknowledgments

I thank Sam's wonderful doctor, Eric Grabowski (Dr. "Bowski" to Sam), who has helped this book along its way. Dr. Candace Erickson has given me a dynamic and profound approach to the physical, psychological, and emotional problems of coping with serious illness. Dr. Anne Moore, too, has given her considerable support to this book.

I know that Sam would want me to thank the many nurses and doctors who helped him and who continue to help children who are seriously ill. They maintain their hope, faith, and love in the midst of great difficulty, and their expertise is a blessing.

In putting together these poems, thanks go first to Molly Peacock, without whom they might never have been written. My debt to Simeon is obvious on every page, and collaborating with him has been one of the great joys in my life.

I am indebted to everyone at CavanKerry Press, particularly to Joan Handler, Ellen Trama, and Sylvia Frezzolini Severance.

This book is a work of love, and so I thank everyone in Sam's extended family. Their love for Sam and for me has been deeply sustaining. My in-laws' generosity and patience this past year allowed me to complete the manuscript. To the many friends who have given their time and love to Sam, to me, and to my family—my eternal gratitude.

To Robert Fagles—many, many thanks. Earl Miner's support, too, has been indispensable.

Finally, I thank my husband, Bill, and my son, Will, for their constant love. Bill, in an act of utter bravery and commitment, sat with me by Sam's bedside in the long months before Sam's death, and when Will came along, with him came the profoundest comfort. I know, wherever Sam is right now, he rejoices in his little brother.

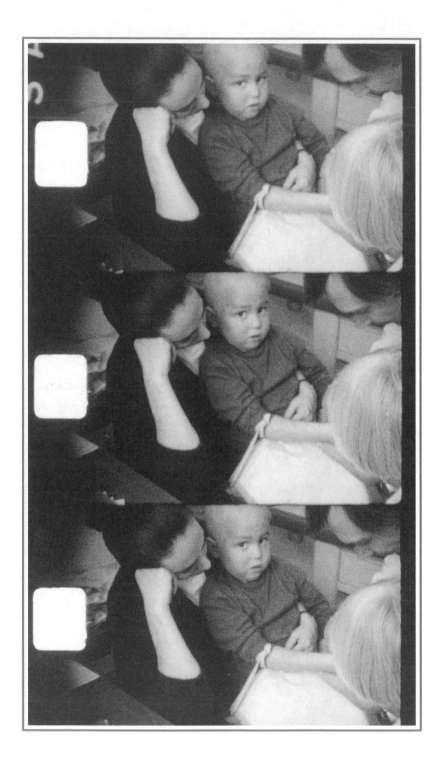

Photographer's Acknowledgments

I wish to thank Cynthia Morris for providing the facilities and equipment for me to begin making digital prints of the photographs for *Life with Sam*.

A residency at the MacDowell Colony in Peterborough, New Hampshire, was invaluable to completing the manuscript, and I am indebted to these fellow colonists for their astute comments on the work: Katherine Min, Mako Yoshikawa, Shyam Salvaduri, Kimberley Hart, Joe Swayze, Andrea Cohen, and Maureen Stanton.

Liz and I also benefited from the critical eyes of my friends Jeff Nachmanoff, Andrew Hildick-Smith, Jennifer Kaufman, and especially Lucy Epstein.

Gail Harriman's unflagging enthusiasm and insight encouraged and guided me from the beginning, while the wise and caring Paul Kaufman provided much needed practical support and advice. And it was Molly Peacock who first suggested that what Liz and I thought might make a good magazine piece could actually be a book. Without her, *Life with Sam* would not have been made.

My deepest gratitude, of course, is to Liz, whose warmth, love, and generosity of spirit helped make this one of the most rewarding experiences I have ever had.

Thanks also to John Perino, at the Focus Gallery in San Francisco, California, where I printed the majority of the photographs for the book, and to West Coast Imaging, which produced digital prints of the images that originated on Super 8 film.

Note from the Publisher

Life with Sam is the inaugural collection of CavanKerry's new imprint—LaurelBooks—fine collections of poetry and prose that explore in depth the many poignant issues associated with confronting serious physical and/or psychological illness.

CavanKerry is grateful to the Arnold P. Gold Foundation for the Advancement of Humanism in Medicine for joining us in sponsoring this new imprint. Offering LaurelBooks as teaching tools to medical schools is the result of mutual concerns—humanism, community and reaching out to the underserved. In concert with the Gold Foundation, CavanKerry's two outreach efforts, GiftBooks and Presenting Poetry and Prose, will bring complimentary books and readings to the medical community at major hospitals.